T0157258

ABUSES'
POETIC
PRODUCT

Ninety pages of printed proof
that negative experiences can
produce positive power.

Marlaina McEachin

authorHOUSE®

AuthorHouse™
1663 Liberty Drive
Bloomington, IN 47403
www.authorhouse.com
Phone: 1-800-839-8640

First published by AuthorHouse 07/27/2011

ISBN: 978-1-4634-1879-3 (sc)
ISBN: 978-1-4634-1880-9 (e)

Library of Congress Control Number: 2011910742

Printed in the United States of America

*Any people depicted in stock imagery provided by Thinkstock are models,
and such images are being used for illustrative purposes only.
Certain stock imagery © Thinkstock.*

This book is printed on acid-free paper.

*Because of the dynamic nature of the Internet, any web addresses or
links contained in this book may have changed since publication and
may no longer be valid. The views expressed in this work are solely those
of the author and do not necessarily reflect the views of the publisher,
and the publisher hereby disclaims any responsibility for them.*

Dedications

I would like to dedicate this book to the memory of my aunt, Martha Carol Hurley. There wasn't a week-end that passed that she didn't have me under her wing reading to me everything imaginable, from the cradle on up. She was an educator in every sense of the word. Martha Carol Hurley, I miss and love you still, Nana Jane.

In addition, I'd like to give thanks to the following edu-cators who positively influenced me and gave me the confidence to pursue my dream publication. Special Thanks to: Mrs. Donna Daniel McCord, Mrs. Michelle May, Dr. Darrell May, and Mr. Robert Wigley.

And, last but not least I would like to dedicate this book to my 6th grade reading teacher, Mrs. Dawson. She is the single most influential person when it comes to me and my writing. She believed in me when I didn't believe in myself and her soothing words got me through some very trying times. I feel that if it weren't for her I wouldn't be where I am today. Mrs. Judy Dawson, to you I am forever in debt. Thank you, I love you! Marlaina

CONTENTS

Often times one may find it to be true,

that surrendering may win the battle too.

-Marlaina McEachin

Introduction

A confession from the author.

Through all the years and all the tears I spent pouring my heart out on paper, it only recently occurred to me that I wasn't just writing. I ran for pen and paper like one would chase down their dearest friend. I ran to it out of anger, I ran to it for companionship, and I ran to it for solace. But, at this stage in my life, after all that I have succumb to, after all that I have overcome, I realize most of all that I ran to my pen and paper for therapy. Had it not been for the ability God gave me for emotions to flow from heart to paper, I'd have probably long since lost my sanity.

My wish for my readers is this...If you can identify with even one of my poems, know that you are not alone. Know that you never were alone, and never will be again. If you have a problem share it with someone, get help. If you have a dirty secret please, oh please tell it. You never know how many more lives you could be affecting. And, always remember no matter how bad it seems today, there is always tomorrow. Regardless of what anyone else says you are worth loving. Never forget to love yourself!

Thank you.

Chapter 1

ABUSE IN ITS MENTAL/ EMOTIONAL FORM

"WHAT LOVE DOESN'T FEEL LIKE"

Realists

Afraid of death yet, intimidated by life.

The world is hard and we are consumed by strife.

Often unable to overcome --

our authoritative figures never succumb.

Many times mislead and many times abused

we are obsequious and are too often used.

We feel no pain and are not afflicted,

our troubled minds grow more demented.

We face each day with new confusions,

no false hopes or candy-coated illusions.

We face life's facts and bitter truths;

pessimistic we stand aloof.

When lightning crashes and we're surrounded by thunder

our hearts are the shelters that we are hidden under.

Alone is how we face our days,

and our live are consistent, it's no longer a phase.

To hope for change would be ludicrous,

personal change has proved to me this.

What were once innocent and impressionable minds

are now unimpressed by the signs of our times.

Our subconscious is all that is filled with laughter;

awaiting a change, forever after.

Faith

Fair-weather friends do not account

for the pain that they cause...abundance is the amount.

They're there when you need them up until the end,

of the time they need you, you're then no longer their friend.

They're there for the laugher and all of the good times,

but their worth to you can be shown in "weathered" times.

When times get hard and you need their support, this is
when you discover that they're no friend of any sort.

With your back turned to them there you stand

yet, then they'll be there knife in hand.

Count on them yes, trust them in full,

your friend they will be instigating a duel.

A friend on this earth can no longer be found,

it's much like a deaf man searching for sound.

This thing you search for is nonexistent,

your trust in that person is inconsistent.

A lesson we learn from this wicked game,

to trust anyone else would be simply insane.

The Quilt

Desperation, abandonment and pain,

tears would fall like pouring rain.

If only the tears hadn't dried

from all the pain I've kept inside.

Answers can't be found in these traumatized days filled
with miseries.

Each day a brand new reason is found for hating life; my
inspiration has drowned.

New agonies and lies are discovered each day

and, regardless of progress they stay.

Haunting my every waking hour,

forcing my heart to grow even more sour.

My initiative has gone to waste;

life's sweet opportunities I no longer taste.

Trapped inside my mind with guilt,

the pattern extends much like a quilt.

Each design portrays in detail

all of my mistakes and defines how I've failed.

Revealing to the world my worth

this quilt of darkness smothers the earth.

So, on I go with no destination

suffering from emotional starvation.

My heart and my stomach quiver in fear;

wondering if I shall see my next year.

Optimism is no longer possessed,

while I am consumed by painful unrest.

Innocence is what I crave,

and will do so until I reach my grave.

Forever will I regret

some decisions I've made when met.

The paths I've chosen have all been wrong turns,

and for this reason my soul burns.

Dreaded is each forthcoming day,

for in misery is the state I stay.

Chamber of Solitude

So many times I'm reminded, and so often I forget

that the only things I yearn for are the things that I can't get

Indulging myself in sorrow and pity,

the tears on my cheek become dry and gritty.

Wishing for happiness, weeping from pain;

from my viewpoint there is nothing to gain.

I defeat my own purpose and dilute my own mind,

therefore creating a prison of solid confines.
I may never discover a way out of this maze,

and therefore, I become more demented and crazed.

My reflection is one of misery and sorrow;

the epitome of yesterdays and the epitome of tomorrows.

This disposition has become a companion to me,

it is in it that I find warmth and security.

Trapped in a chamber of morbid confusion,

I have the eyes of a drunk and see only delusion.

My spouse of darkness provides serenity,

in my comatose state I find tranquility.

I now re-enter my cell of solitude and silence,

escaping a world filled with burdens and violence.

Brief was my departure and antisocial was my stay;

The enthusiasm for my future has been forever locked away.

Love

As I drift through my dreams and sift through my thoughts,

I envision your image and the last time that we fought.

That day ended all of my bravery, yet it took away my fears;

As the nurse attempted to soothe my mind, she said
"they'd" give you years.

I know that you were justified in the actions that you've taken.

You swore you'd never hurt me, so "they" must be mistaken.

This was all overdramatized, simply misunderstood.

If you'd only come to visit, I'd forgive you, yes I would.

They think that I can't hear them as they speak of my condition.

While the entire time I'm analyzing and reliving my rendition.

I remember when you raised your fist, screamed at me
and swore,

but on the ambulance you whispered, "it will not happen anymore."

I know your words are true and I abide by them as law.

I promise I will not press charges, I'll say it was a fall.

I love you no matter what and I'd testify in court

that we've never had an argument or a fight of any sort.

To see you smile with pleasure and pull my body near,

I can imagine the entire scene, it's all so plain and clear.

Imagine however, is all that I can do, for I've lost my sight completely

They've rinsed away the blood and sewn my gashed up neatly.

It probably sounds painful, but it didn't hurt a bit.

My entire body will move no more; I'm able only to sit.

Don't you blame yourself my dear, for you and I both know,

that you would never hurt me, if you didn't <u>love</u> me so.

Affliction

It feels as though I'm falling into a pit that has no end.

I'm offered aid by a helping hand, yet my hand -- to weak to lend.

So, there I lay on the floor

my entire body spasmatic, shaken to the core.

It's a burden, it's a shame, it's an embarrassment.

I despise this affliction and I believe that it's "hell-sent."

There's no cure, no explanation, and no end in sight.

Once I sense that it's approaching I'm consumed by a horrific fright.

It makes me nervous and detains my life.

I feel as though I am condemned by this overwhelming strife.

The neurologists seem as if my case is a mere formality,

yet my uncontrollable quivering is an abnormality.

I know this isn't normal, and I know it isn't fair,

to awaken from these bodily tremors and be faced with anxious stares.

Everyone rushes over and everyone is interested

in my mortal humiliation, now more gossip can be spread.

I'm not whining for attention or asking for sympathy.

I'm simply describing my experiences with epilepsy.

Creators

We begin untouched and uninfluenced. We grow and in this growth we gain. What we gain is experience, experience and knowledge. From these we gain opinions and lessons. From our lessons we learn. We learn to make decisions. It is in these decisions that we determine; determine our own futures. We create our own destinies and our own fates. We are creators. Creators of either success of failure. Therefore, we are in essence creating the life in which we intend to live. There is no one in which to blame.

No one person other than ourselves who can be justifiably blamed for our achievement, or lack thereof. We ourselves, and only ourselves, can be held accountable. Our mentors may teach and our peers may influence, but we are the only credible indicator of our life. In conclusion, we end as we began, untouched and uninfluenced. In the aspect of accountability we are creators.

Playground

Ample confusion;

more than is needed.

I create a delusion;

hallucinations are feeded.

Further away goes reality.

As my mind renders images,

I lose personality.

I break for momentary visits

on few occasions

into the "real world"

which cause mental abrasions.

I reenter my personal

sanctuary with great anticipation.

My mind is my amusement

I am my recreation.

She

She was with many.

She had such a selection.

She was with many,

despite all suggestions.

She was with many,

she went in cycles.

She was with many,

she had no rivals.

She was with many.

She was a scandal.

She was with many,

Her life...a fading candle.

She was with many,

her health was fleeting.

She was with many,

the rumor was leaking.

She was with many.

She spends her days crying.

She was with many.

Now, she lays dying.

Solitary

There's no drug, no amount of alcohol, no state of delusion which provides comfort. I am always uptight, awkward-desolate. Never do I feel as though I belong. No bond between myself and another is strong enough for confidence...trust. I can never reveal my true self. I am constantly on guard, for people are always on, "the look-out" for the vulnerable ones. The ones to take advantage of. I am solitary...forever alone.

Silence

I can't explain my silence.

I feel awkward...insecure.

I can't explain my silence.

I feel tainted and impure.

I can't explain my silence.

I wouldn't if I could.

I can't explain my silence.

It would be too personal, maybe I should?

I can't explain my silence.

Too much truth may give me away.

I can't explain my silence.

I'll speak with you some other day.

Demise

Each day I awaken I die.

Each breath I breathe, I die.

Each hour that passes, I die.

Being social, making friends, pursuing

an education for a promising future all

is all in vain.

To please the world,

to satisfy the judgmental minds of others

is no longer a priority.

The American dream of a

happy home-a husband-a few kids-

is no longer a conceivable notion.

For I have realized that from the moment

I was conceived I have been dying.

Without ever being exposed to illness,

without ever being reckless,

without ever being born-we die.

Last Days

Waiting and wondering; passing the time.

Knowing that this is just another sign.

-A sign of the times we are in,

a time of betrayal, a time of sin.

-A time of unexpectedness, yet

harsh reality, a time of punishment.

-A time that we will not forget.

-A time that we have brought upon ourselves.

-A time that is certainly meant.

A test that God is giving, one I wonder if we can pass...

for, this test is given to us all the same, in the days which will be our last.

Materialism

I look around, and what do I see?

Humans in oblivion wanting everything for free.

Sure, they work hard and deserve things they earn.

However, liability for their actions they make no attempt to learn.

Oh, how I loathe being redundant, but wanting the world for free!

I simply can't comprehend it, perhaps that is just me.

Possibly, I am the one who is wrong. Who am I to interpret?

According to the majority, its true I am the culprit!

Change my ways, my outlook, or perhaps my disposition?

The whole idea is preposterous! To even consider this inquisition.

I suppose that I will remain lonesome in this, my values, and perception.

However, morals were once instilled and practiced, to my recollection.

Despite the social seclusion and all the friendships that its cost

in reveling in the materialism - they will pay the highest price.

They are the ones who have lost.

America the Beautiful

Americans are able to open every door.

We discover many things and still we search for more.

Each door we open with no convictions.

We ignore all orders and moral restrictions.

We're confident, determined, and so dreadfully eager

to be the first to experience...we yearn to be leaders.

We all want to be different, and we all think that we are unique,

yet we prove ourselves wrong each time we speak.

We hate others, as well as condemn,

and are eager to inflict pain on a whim.

We the people of the United States

have ruined many lives and sealed many fates.

It is disappointing to know that the country in which we live,

is willing to offer, and yet not give.

Our entire foundation is based on lies,

the condemnation, the judgment, nor the hate in our
hearts will ever die.

We're cruel, we're harsh, and willing to kill

Over material things, forsaking lives; these wars; surreal.

The heart of society has long since stopped beating,

and faith in our constitution is depleting.

Procrastination

So many things keep me from writing:

time, people, emotions, the pen.

So many things keep us from heaven:

time, people, emotions, sin.

Procrastination is a curse to man

that can keep successes from making its stand.

If you allow it...it will dominate

and a failure of you it can create.

Take control...make a stand.

Of your fate, you're at the command.

Each day matters, no action is in vain.

Complete each task without disdain.

Procrastination is waiting for your mistake;

while your future is waiting for you to create.

Accordance

When I awake on each new day sometimes I almost seethe.

Seethe with anger and bitterness to find that I'm still here.

To bring to you face such disgust.

I don't want or wish for a ripe old age.

I don't wish for one more year.

I no longer have motivation for moving ahead in life.

In fact, I focus more on avoiding it.

I only hope that my time here is not limited by my own accordance.

Chapter 2

ABUSE IN ITS PHYSICAL FORM

"WHAT LOVE DOESN'T FEEL LIKE"

I'm 17

I hate it, I despise it.

It being how I feel when you cast your domineering voice upon me.

Weakening me, it casts me back into my childhood and I'm reminded once again of how feeble and fragile not only my body is, but my state of mind as well.

I'm forced back into a world of fear and contempt; contempt for my life and my surroundings.

Forced to face what I've so securely locked away, locked away for so long the misery I suffered.

Yet, by one tone of your forceful and anger-induced voice I am reminded.

I am forced to reflect upon a force that cannot be reckoned with...memory.

I being lunged back am faced with all the terror a youth's mind can contain.

Memories obtained by the abuse that was received.

It is from these memories which I run, attempting to forget that the past ever happened.

It is through this self-inflicted amnesia that I and my mind remain stable, sane.

My sanity obtained through denial.

Is this insane?

I think not.

For, as long as I do not remember, it never really happened.

So, if it didn't happen, am I normal?

Is there any such thing?

Of course there is a normal state of mind which is exactly what I can sustain if you're quiet.

Don't yell, I hate it when you yell.

I think I might cry.

However, as long as you are monotone I can maintain my actual age.

Shh, as long as you're quiet I'm 17.

Silent Resentment

I am mute.

I do not speak.

No one can hear me.

This situation is bleak.

I grow tired of being patronized.

No one hears my silent cry.

Many times I close my eyes and welcome the chance to die.

I despise the constant bickering going on inside.

There is no chance for me to escape, for from myself I cannot hide.

I will continue my withdrawal; my only associate is me.

I've grown to hate the life I lead, and I resent my identity.

Chance

I've analyzed everyone that I know.

The more I try to hide it, the more my anger shows.

It's time to point the accusatory finger at myself.

For, I'm the one I hate.

While I've torn everyone else's character apart,

I've destroyed all that there was of my heart;

or hidden at least; perhaps from myself...

put all real emotion upon someone else.

I've abandoned everyone including my mind.

I wonder where I am. Am I lost in time?

Reminiscing of a time when I was done wrong;

get over that, get past that, you're grown.

Numb is how I feel and dumb is what I am.

I take everything for granted as if tomorrow I will be handed,

another chance, another day, another breath to scoff away.

Devotional

For all of the years that I endured your cruel,

slanderous, and insensitive drool...
For all of the years I underwent the thrashing,

the bashing, the punishment...

For all of the childhood that you stole from me

that has been locked away lonely, for eternity...

For all of the tears that I've sat and cried

and all of the hate that dwells inside...

For all of the secrets that you've kept from me

and all of the sins that you introduced to me.

The only thing that I have to say,

is you know who you are...but I love you anyway.

Image

Do you run past mirrors?

Or, can you stand and face the image in which has so nearly been erased?

Erased by the deeds in which you've done...

done to the one whom you should love.

You carried this child within for nine months.

You bore, she bled, she cried, she fled.

Now, never again shall you see this child.

Nor, the image that faded all those years that you lied.

Familiar Compassion

That little girl lost so long ago haunts me more and more.

It no longer matters where I'm at, at home, at the store.

She can strike at any time, to embarrass me is her passion.

I present this phisode; she shows up, destroying it with familiar compassion.

That same familiar compassion that was once shown to her.

But, what I don't understand is why she takes it out on me!

I was there! I was her! What gives her this right?

The right to come back after all these years and torture me again.

If she'd only stop screaming, stop crying, stop hating me, I'd be her friend.

At least...I'd try. I'd hold her, console her, tell her everything's alright.

Because there would never be another bloody, bruised, or tearful night.

What do I do with this hate-filled child that has grown up yet tortures me?

When all she has ever wanted was love and will not take it from me.

Flood

Nightmares...sweaty.

Should I cry?

Too often wondered

how will I die.

Memories flood me,

sounds as well.

Nightmare?

Reality?

How do I tell?

Confusion...ample!

Why God?

Why?

I panic when tears well...

what if I cry?

To sleep renders memory.

Amnesia return!

Have I truly forgiven?

My soul...will it burn?

Flashbacks...they flood back.

My mother's safety I cradle.

Recollection,

I shut out

now I am able.

No sleep for the weary.

Age cannot elude this.

To function normally,

completely ludicrous!

Only a child,

too young to suffer.

Where was God?

Where was mother?

Broken nose, busted skin,

My strong phisode crumbles within.

How dare I reveal this?

But, if not now, then when?

To confide this

pure betrayal.

Perhaps, even a sin.

Little Girl

No matter how I try to help, no matter what I do,

nothing seems to satisfy, I give my all...I submit to you.

You are my father, you are my daddy.

I will always try to please, to win the affection or even
acceptance of the one man that owns me.

I know more than anyone how many times I've failed,

and despite how much I try it seems, that I never will prevail.

I'm sure that this is part of the penance that I must pay,

for the sins in my past, that God was judging every day.

But, what about all the moments, days, weeks, months
and years?

What about that little girl's admiring eyes, so often filled
with tears.

Those days came long before my life went so awry.

So, I ask you now, where's that little girl who longs for
love and reassurance, who deep inside still cries?

For, she wants only to please you no matter what her cost.

And by neglecting that long lost little girl, that young lady
is long lost.

The Babysitter, The Boy, or The Man

He cuffs his hands beneath her chin,

explains to her how to begin.

Not more than five, she complied in fear.

He whispers his dirty desires in her tiny ear.

He unzips his fly, he pulls out his sin.

It's been 21 years, yet she still can't trust men.

He grasps the back of this child's head,

pulls it forward...whispers, "just do what I said."

He reminds her how dirty this secret is, and how dirty
she is as well.

She knows that he is right, she fears she'll burn in hell.

So she keeps his secret, only now is it exposed.

But, where was the babysitter, his mother, do you suppose?

Conveniently, she disappeared on each of these occasions.

I'd like to think she never knew about each brutal mental
abrasion.

The only regret I have in keeping my silence, is now that teenage boy is a man...with two daughters, I understand.

My only concern is whose loving these girls? The babysitter, the boy, or the man.

Chapter 3

ABUSE IN THE FORM OF DRUG USE

"WHAT LOVE DOESN'T FEEL LIKE"

Loss

People surround me, but I'm here alone.

My body is here, but my mind is gone.

Unhappiness plagues me despite my location.

Regardless of my goals, I have no destination.

I smile, I laugh, and I try to compensate

For my underlying problems, an illusion I create.

Deeper and deeper my problems are imbedded

and the mere thought of dealing with them is dreaded.

To please everyone else is my primary concern,

their respect and adoration is what I attempt to earn.

While the entire time I'm unable to see

That only pleasing others is killing only me.

Not a single person satisfied with the actions that I've taken,

I thought that I was a necessity, so I must be mistaken.

So much time is spent comforting those who are in need,

that my problems only deepen -- never to be freed.

The People

I hate them, I hate their lies.

You can smell their deceit, you can see their dilated eyes.

It's all fiction, it's all insincere.

You either become one of them, or you live in fear.

Join the crowd...become one of us.

Discard your morals, don't make a fuss.

Make it easy.

Don't put up a fight.

You've become one of the demons.

You've lost, alright!

They have consumed you.

You now contribute to the evil.

Prepare to burn.

You're one of the people.

Faithful Day

I don't know where I'm headed, and will never admit to
where I've been

There's no excuse for my behavior; there's no repentance
for the way I've sinned

Given the chance I'd change most anything concerning my
decisions

For, in this faulty life I've lead, I have an extended list of
revisions

Regret hovers above my head for everyone to see,

And while I act as though it's them that I hate, I know I'm
hating me

I disgust myself day to day, yet each tomorrow is the same

Regardless of whom it is I accuse, I'm the one whose
earned the blame

I've known the consequences of each action that I've
taken,

And each time that I have sought rebellion it has been my
character that was forsaken

Wondering who I am, knowing who I could be,

I look into my mirror and realize I'm just me.

This discouraging fact I face each and every day,

Yet each new day I pattern after the previous ones that have slipped away

Excuses I use will satisfy my conscience until that fateful day arrives,

When my soul is released from a body that has deceased and my heart no longer thrives

Self

I feel as though I've lost.

I've participated in a relentless battle and my soul has been the cost.

It's gone, it has disappeared, I'm numb.

I was unaware of the battle until it was over, and due that I feel dumb.

When did this dreadful battle ensue?

Why did it happen? What didn't I do?

What could I have possibly done to suffer such a loss?

Who was the invisible opponent who's hung my soul upon a cross?

I ask these questions as if someone else may know,

how it is I could lose myself and never even know.

Maybe there wasn't a battle at all. Maybe I threw my soul away.

Maybe that's not the case; at least I hope it's not...I pray.

God, give me the strength to face my fears, find myself, repent!

Discover my calling, and my soul, and the reason for which I've been sent.

To make a positive influence, to touch someone within,

to take a stand for my beliefs, and relieve myself from sin.

Resignation

Decisions I've made against everyone's will,

I was determined to do it for only a thrill.

I thought it was invigorating, daring and brave.

Now, its distance and amnesia that my mind craves.

I want out and to escape this condemning hole,

for without success and respect I have no soul.

I wish to forget my daring deeds.

For, it's on rumors and failure that this community feeds.

It would be great to escape condemnation,

But do expect such exclusion from "Grand Gossip Station?" No!

I got what I earned, I deserve every bit.

From the mouths of my comrades I receive only spit.

I'm forced to tolerate the additional lies,

and grow tired of creating alibis.
I'm through, I'm finished, and never again will I pursue it.

I'm done, I resign. But sadly, I blew it!

Carry On

At least once in our lives we meet a "friend,"

someone who needs us, just as we need them.

We love our "friend" and trust them too.

There is nothing, for these souls, that we wouldn't do!

We grow dependant on this relationship, taking for
granted that it might end.

We pull out all stops and our hearts we extend.

Inevitably something happens, bringing this duo to an end.

We find ourselves confused and speechless. They were
our "friends," how could they do this?

Not only have we lost our "friend," but a part of our-
selves as well.

Exactly how much we have shared with this person we
are ashamed to tell.

In ignorance, we gave our all to another, that would des-
ert us, and all that we did share.

We awake from this misery to find that they will not be
back, nor do they care.

How we manage is up to us.

Do we pick up the pieces? Have a meltdown? Curse? No!

We carry ourselves with dignity, regardless of the pain.

We face humiliation with poise and restrain.

We leave to honor ourselves above those "friends,"

And stop seeking security provided by sin.

We become stronger individuals. Stronger than we knew,

And achieve self-respect, all things we can do.

Evil

What will I do when evil approaches?

What will I do when he is near?

Will I run away and hide?

Will I stand up and face my fear?

Will I revert back to my fetal stage?

Will I fall down upon the floor, suck my thumbs or act my age?

Will I call for daddy, or simply cry,

or close my eyes and wish to die?

Will I draw my knife and hold my own?

Or stand there dazed and in a zone?

Where will I go? What will I do?

And what will you do, when he comes for you?

Lost

To witness so much promise turn into shame.

To be perfectly conscious of who is to blame.

To imagine all things that just might have been,

turn into lies, humiliation and sin.

To remember a life that was once so at peace,

and awake to one filled with addiction and grief.

To comprehend the problem and call it by name,

and return to the demon and relive your shame.

Leads one to question, how lost are they?

To be so close to the problem, yet so far away.

Far from the solution that lay just before them. For, it is
up to us to decide who we are.

If we are uncertain, then we are dangerously far.

Far from becoming who we once were,

then try and fathom that we are not sure!

We must search both our minds and our souls deep within,

And retrieve those people whose bodies we're in.

He sends solutions for us day by day.

It is up to us, His people, to find Him as their way.

Why Wake?

The anger, the hatred, the acceptance of fear,

My stomach turns, my curiosity yearns to learn why I am still here?

Why didn't it work? Why did I not succeed? The concept is simple, just do the right thing.

Now my soul swims in loneliness and a melody of guilt is the tune my heart sings.

To live in this state is much more dreaded than death.

I plunder, I search for the end, and my last breath.

If only there were some way to repent...

I've prayed, I've pleaded for my soul to be sent...

To relieve everyone else of my presence is what I long to achieve.

Resting in silence, near my father, sweet relief.

But, even there my selfishness reigns,

while consciousness plagues me each morning that I wake.

Epiphany

We don't understand why some people insist on making
decisions to put them at risk. This foolish game that they
insist on playing

keeps their life stationary, this is where they're staying.

No matter how we try to reason and explain to them the truth,

they stand adamantly ignorant and aloof.

It seems just in spite of our simple requests and pleadings,

they strive harder to defy regardless of the voices bleating.

It also seems that in knowing this we'd give up and let it be.

However, with failure and self-destruction we will never agree.

Beg and plead we might, nag and ourselves we despite,
giving up we'll never do, we're fighters just as they.

If all our efforts fail, perhaps we'll stop and pray.

Chapter 4

ABUSE OF THE HEART

"WHAT LOVE DOESN'T FEEL LIKE"

Opportunity Missed

The passion that dwells within me forever will remain

a secret and a burden, my heart is filled with pain.

I may never know the touch of love or the comfort of
happiness,

but briefly was my heart content and never will I forget this.

The most satisfying times of my life have already taken place.

I wonder what I should look forward to, I've already
experienced grace.

The one I love and adore will never even know the im-
portance of his existence; he owns my heart and more.

Never did I tell him and forever will I regret the loss of
opportunity and the love I'll never get.

Unintentional Distributions

Each time that I envision you or see your smiling face

my heart feels as if it's no longer there and ice is in its place.

Your love would mean so much to me, what I'd give to know
you care,

but love I fear is something that you and I will never share.

This you'd think would discourage me; disgrace and humiliate,

but my heart know no boundaries, therefore doom is my
only fate.

I seek the pain that you distribute, I hunger for even more.

I'd give you up and seek another, but its agony that I adore.

Your distributions are unintentional even you are unaware,

of the pain and suffering I receive simply because I care.

The Cycle

To love is to lose.

To live is to love.

To trust is to be deceived.

To love is to trust.

To live is to suffer.

To live is to love.

To love is to be alone.

To live is to lose.

Last Night

It had been months since I'd seen your face,

held your hand, or felt your embrace,

I spoke to you briefly on the phone,

and discovered something that I hadn't known.

Yours is the voice that comforts me,

opens my eyes and allows me to see.

Yours is the heart that when we meet,

mends my soul and makes me complete.

You are the owner of so many traits

that convince me so that you are my soul mate.

I'm sorry to say that my realization came too late,

for that conversation determined my fate.

You said you were happier than ever before,

and you held in your hand the key to a door.

The door to a home built for two.

Immediately, I asked whom?

Without hesitation you asked in delight,

"Didn't you know I was married last night?"

My heart shattered and fell to the floor,

but I could say no more.

Don't be surprised when you learn of my death,

for I wrote you this message with my last breath.

When you receive this letter I now ask you in delight,

"Didn't you know I died last night?"

Thorny Wall

There's a thorny wall around it,

excitement may cause it to swell.

There's a thorny wall around it,

and if it's punctured it will fail.

There's a thorny wall around it

that keeps me in place.

There's a thorny wall around it

that protects it like a brace.

There's a thorny wall around it

that keeps me locked inside,

and if you ever wish to find me

it's behind this thorny wall I hide.

Irony

The closer I get to another the further I withdraw.

Snuggling deep within my nest of familiar comfort.

The moment I feel that I could release and become part of something...my senses rebel.

Once again I withdraw. Reaching the dark recesses of my personal sanctuary, feel the tension release...knowing that once again I am safe.

The feeling of companionship which I seek from another, I flee at the sight of.

The person that could very well rescue me from my misery I shun.

And the very place within me in which I seek shelter drives me to the point of insanity.

Lesson

It was love that taught me to be emotionless, cold and unconcerned.

It was love that shamed me, took my pride, and a lesson I did learn.

It was love that taught me never to be involved in a relationship requiring my heart to enter.

It was love that taught me to be a borrower and never to be a lender.

It was love that taught me that one is never reciprocated for all that they are giving.

It was love and the lack thereof, that taught me that without it there is no living.

Death of a Daisy

She was vibrant.

She was strong.

Until a strange wind came along.

She was twisted.

She was broken.

Nothing was heard, not a sound spoken.

Deceit

You want me to care, but it would do no good.

You're only going to leave me, like you should.

To your home you go after each session,

creating your next excuse and confession.

I'm here for your convenience and nothing more.

I'm erased from your mind before you reach your front door.

You're seemingly sincere, suave and tender,

but I'll never own you...you're just a lender.

You have obligations and priorities,

and I'm not included in any of these.
I'm only a lie that you have to cover.

I'm not a person, so I'm not your lover.

When you feel secure in your escape from suspsion,

you'll gradually lose interest and pay me no attention.

I know this, expect this, and await each day,

and each day that it continues is a miracle in some way.

You've assumed the role of a man, but you've broken
every rule,

and if you think that I have fallen for you...well then,
you're the fool.

Regretfully Misled

Pardon my ignorance, I misunderstood.

I assumed I could trust you, but you taught me good.

You slandered my name and disgraced my reputation.

I'd just like to thank you for your generous donation.

You've ruined my life and scarred me as well;

I no longer have friends and I'm living in hell.

You've tormented me beyond comprehension,

and I can only assume that it was you're intention.

I'm sorry I met you and regretfully I say

that I hope someone does you the same damn way.

Tarnished Armor

I thought that you were different...my "Knight in shining armor."

I misjudged your character as well as your karma.

From the moment we met you've told nothing but fiction.

I've often wondered, was it an attempt or addiction.

I've tried to understand, listen and forgive.

However, repetitive sins I refuse to forgive.

You've taken advantage of my tender young mind for as long as I'll allow you.

You've proven untrustworthy and manipulative in everything you do.

You've played your impetuous games, fallen from my graces and lost my respect.

However, knowing the measurements of your ego I assume that that has no effect.

Your under the impression that your superior to all.

However, someone should remind you that the highest-- hardest fall.

Someday soon you will learn your lesson, reap what you

sew, and be compensated,

for your unacceptable behavior as well as those with
whom you've "related."

You will be ignored, you will be patronized.

Because of your scandalous behavior, your pathological lies.

You and I

I think about you even now…the times we shared, even after all that's happened.

I suppose I'll always think of you.

Maybe a part of me will always want you. Knowing that I never really had you makes me curious.

I wonder how things could have been.

I know that I loved you, and I know that I still do.

I also know that that doesn't bring conclusion to anything, if anything it only complicates things.

Especially my mind.

Regardless of who I'm with or what I'm doing, I still think of you.

It's the little things that bring you back to haunt me.

The songs we shared, the season in which we met, the remarks that you made that I recognize in someone else's jargon.

Nevertheless, it's you who are with me each day, and you who will never want me and it is you and I who will never be.

Your Eyes and the Roses

I didn't understand you yet I attempted to believe,

and each time that I was convinced was one more time
that you deceived.

I would have left at the first sign of dishonesty,

but between your eyes and the roses that thought was
un-conceived.

While feeling like a princess so high upon my throne,

I had forgotten all the rules that previously I had known.

I forgot to be suspicious and I forgot to investigate,

and for my royal delusion pain was my fate.

Cry

Even after all she had seen a lesson she failed to learn.

Even after all the times she swore in Hell he'd burn.

The world still turning, her eyes still burning; she escaped
to the man who would love her.

Only to find her soul intertwined with that of the evil other.

She had become the one that she hated.

Was it because her wounds were outdated?
Did her mind and her body yearn for the punishment that
previously it did know?

And if she was without it, who was she? And where was
she to go?

So, she turns the bitterness inside out and directs it to-
wards her lover.

But, his heart is good; he is like no other.

This contradicts everything she's seen and she under-
stands not why,

a man could simply love her...not love to see her cry.

The Rain

The rain is coming and it looks heavy.

The rain is coming. Will it break the levy?

Through the course of its showers if in fact;

it should over power the two in its path.

Who is to blame?

The weakest of the two holds the shame.

I will be strong, I will put up a fight.

A raft - a rope - an anchor?

I will hold on tight!

The rain is coming.

Can we swim?

Relief in Not Knowing

It seems lately that I am baffled, star struck and or confused.

I know that I am the recipient of love but, I fear that I am being used.

I feel as though it is a crime to experience such emotion.

Therefore, I deny what he has offered; his devotion.

No one could be in love with me, happy or satisfied.

I live in solitude, in melancholy I reside.

I wonder why he is here and I question his motives for staying.

Let me escape before he hurts me, this is all that I am praying.

I am to faulty and obviously flawed for his pure and honest intentions.

Or is this facade that he portrays a devious invention?

I want to believe and I yearn to trust, but I find that I am incapable of trusting and accepting the affection of others, for I myself am unacceptable.

So, how am I to tell "the one" I love, who is perfect in every way that still I am unhappy and he must go away?

I must free him from his fate and save his heart from grief

to lift my presence from his life will be an eventual relief.

I love him more than he will ever know but, I have no
known way of showing,

therefore, I shall set him free without him ever knowing.

Silence

Too often it isn't mutual, one consumed with the other;

the other consumed with another.

Never are the feelings equal.

So much has been shared.

Yet, so much is left to be desired.

You are looked upon as a friend, and this angers you.

You yearn to be so much more.

Yet, here you are listening and learning.

Learning more about the one you desire.

Yet, sinking farther and farther into that endless pit
labeled confidant.

Friendship is great and you feel flattered to have as much.

Yet, what's missing goes much deeper.

Your relationship is strictly verbal,

and physical attributes are what you crave.

You question your own tendencies; and wonder if they're wrong.

Knowing that the warm caresses in which you wish to

share may

quite possibly drive away what you so long to touch.
And this representing everything in opposition of what you

wish to achieve becomes what you withhold.

It lingers and fizzles and nearly disappears.

Every emotion you've ever had dies with you in your silence.

My Mate

I despise this feeling of solitude.

I am constantly seeking the end.

I wish to find a companion, a lover, and a friend.

All of this, I seek in one man,

honest and willing by me to stand.

Each day I venture out, I pursue my quest.

Yet, time after time each man fails the test.

My search is for the one whose eyes would never stray.

Yet, each flunkey I leave behind, in dismay.

Until I stumble upon my treasure that awaits;

I'll continue the search for my friend, my mate.

So Much Better

To be true to you is all that I know.

To be fair to you, would be to let you go.

To spare you the disease that is my pain,

the perpetual denial, distrust and blistered muscle that
once was my brain.

I would wish this on no one, not even an enemy.

To force it upon you would be criminal of me.

I love you, of that I am sure.

That is why you must go.

To drag you into my misery well, I simply refuse to do so.

I'm sorry you had to meet me.

But, I'm so thankful for our time together.

Because, knowing you makes me that much more sure

that you deserve so much better.

Your Chance

With each hour that passed, I trusted you less.

Which only proves me right, I guess.

This doesn't please me, in any way.

I pray that someone proves me wrong, someday!

Someday someone can be honest and true.

Someone can be faithful perhaps, even you!

I hope you can find what your searching for;

a lover, a mate, a companion- a whore.

Whatever it is that your heart desires,

I hope that it's that you find.

For, my mental capacity and depths of my soul require

more than just a "good time."

When you grow older, mature in years;

this is when you'll face your fears.

I will be who you refer to as "the one who got away."

Because only age will provide you with the insight to say...

She was the one who would have stood by my side,

the one who never cheated, the one who never lied.

One day you'll miss me, and I apologize in advance,

for the pain you'll suffer from that realization.

Because you know you had your chance.

In conclusion, I'd like to thank God for all his many blessings. I'd like to thank my mother for always having a positive thought to share. I'd like to thank my brothers for getting me through times that they themselves were unaware of, being my conscience, if you will. Last, but not least, I'd like to thank my significant other for providing me with solid advice and for supporting me. I love you all.